A VERY SCARY PUMPKIN

Story by Jeff Minich
Ilustrated by Renan Garcia

ISBN 978-0-9862224-8-1

With all their toys and
treats packed away

They arrived to find their new home was quite large and looked very old!

Ivy creeped and crawled
along the ground and walls,
ready to grab ahold of everything
including the Nuggies paws!

The house was dusty and dark inside
with lots of places for creatures to hide...

Its wooden floors creaked
and groaned as the Nuggies explored

Little did Chomper and Coco know...

they were being followed everywhere
by a very scary ghost!

Her name was Pumpkin and, like most ghosts,
she preferred living alone!

Fear was her favorite way to control anyone that dared to step into her home.

So she played a mean trick and trapped Chomper and Coco down in the basement!

As the Nuggies tried
to find a way to escape...

...their Daddy searched for them
all over the place.

He looked out back in the dark of night,
only to have Pumpkin lock him outside!

...and didn't think twice about
the poor trapped little Nuggies

So when their Daddy was able
to find a way back in...

... and set Chomper and Coco free.
Pumpkin decided she had to get a lot more scary!

Later that night, after the Nuggies fell asleep,
Pumpkin appeared under a big white sheet

She whirled around and shouted loudly
"This is my house and you all must leave!"

As thunder and lightning struck outside,
Pumpkin used her ghostly powers
to make the Nuggies cower and hide.

But as each bolt of lighting flashed, they realized she wasn't a pumpkin at all.

She was really just the ghost of a cat!

"Raaaaaaarrrr!"
Chomper yelled as he
flew off the bed

"You're not scary!!
You're really JUST...
A .. KIIIITTY!!!!" he said

"Well, actually
I'm the ghost of a kitty"
Pumpkin said softly

"And I can be very
scary if want to ...see?!"

"But why do you want to be so scary?"
Coco wondered

"I was here first
and I like things the way they were!"
Pumpkin told her

"But we'll have to become friends if we're all going to live here!" Chomper sighed

After thinking it over, Pumpkin knew Chomper was right ...

Because being scary meant
she would always be lonely...

and what she really
wanted was to be part of a family!

So each night after that
Pumpkin was a sweet spirited cat
And found a nice place to dream
Curled up right next to the Nuggies!

CPSIA information can be obtained at www.ICGtesting.com
Printed in the USA
LVOW05*0832091015

457352LV00014B/41/P

9 780986 222481